KU-450-514

Catherine Marshall

God loves you

Our Family's Favourite Stories and Prayers

Hodder and Stoughton

London · Sydney · Auckland · Toronto

Printed in West Germany for Hodder and Stoughton
Limited, Mill Road, Dunton Green, Sevenoaks, Kent.
Co-edition by Coprint GmbH, Wiesbaden

The author wishes to express her appreciation to the Estate of Laura E. Richards and to Little, Brown & Company for permission to adapt "The Coming Of The King" from the book THE GOLDEN WINDOWS; to Doubleday & Company, Inc., for permission to adapt for "The Babies Who Wouldn't Eat", twenty-six lines from PEACE IN THE HEART by Archibald Rutledge; to Angelo Patri and to *Young Wings,* the magazine of the Junior Literary Guild, for permission to reprint "The Little Red Wagon"; to Harper & Row for permission to use one sentence from YOUR CHILD AND GOD by Robbie Trent; to Canon Wallace Elliott, for Peter Marshall's adaptation of his benediction; to Grace Hildebrand, Elizabeth Ann Campagna, and Leonora W. Wood for many helpful suggestions; to her two youngest and best critics — Mickey Campagna and Tommy Wharton. "The King with Wet Feet" is based on an English legend, and "The Way of a Crab" on a tale from Aesop.

If there should remain any unacknowledged material in this book, the publisher will welcome word to that effect and will give proper credit in all future editions.

CONTENTS

COME IN — WON'T YOU?

In our home, it has been the custom to have family prayers in the evening right after dinner. Even before the dinner dishes were washed, the whole family would gather in our living room.

"Get comfortable now," Peter John's daddy would say. To Peter John, comfortable meant sitting on a little stool, or lying propped on his elbows on the rug before the open fire. To Jeff, our cocker spaniel, comfortable meant lying contentedly at his master's feet.

Peter-daddy, seated in his big easy chair, would read a bit from the Bible lying open on his knees. Then often he would tell us a story. These stories helped us to understand what God is like and how He wants us to act, so that we may please Him and become His happy, helpful children.

This nicest-time-of-the-whole-day then would be closed with prayer. Peter John's father often told him, "Just talk to God about anything on your mind, Peter John, in your own language, in your own way. That's what prayer is."

7

We thought you would like our family-prayertime stories as much as we like them. That's why Peter John and I decided to make this book. We have included a few of the talking-things-over sort of prayers too.

As you look at and read this book, we hope that you will feel that you are a guest in our home. Friendship is here — and God's love.

Come in — won't you?

THE LITTLE
RED WAGON

In a Western town, there was a little mission church, where the true Christmas spirit still lived. It was the custom there, on Christmas Eve, to put many candles on the altar and, close by, little figures of the Nativity scene. There was the manger in the stable, and Mary and Joseph, the Baby Jesus lying in the straw, and the animals in their stalls. And overhead was the one bright star which guided the Wise Men to Bethlehem.

Early one Christmas morning, the pastor of the church went to see that all the little figures were in place for the first service. He was horrified to see that the tiny figure of the Baby Jesus was gone. The pastor looked everywhere, but he could not find it.
As the pastor left the church, he was almost run over by a little boy racing a red wagon along the pavement.

It was Pierre — the baker's son. The pastor smiled and started to speak to the boy, when, suddenly, he noticed in the red wagon, the missing figure of the Christ Child.

"Pierre!" he cried. "It was *you!* You took the Baby Jesus. Why did you do it?"

Pierre hung his head and was silent. The pastor scolded and questioned. Still Pierre would not explain. He just hung his head and dug the toe of one scuffed shoe into the side of the other.

"It — it was like this," Pierre finally blurted out, "I — I wanted a red wagon for Christmas, and I prayed. I asked Jesus to let me have a red wagon. And — and I promised Him that if I got one, I'd give Him a ride in it. It's His birthday, you know."

The good pastor smiled down at the little boy, and there were tears in his eyes.

"I'm sorry I scolded, Pierre. I didn't understand. You are quite right. It *is* His birthday, and you have given Him the nicest gift of all."

11

THANK YOU, GOD, FOR LITTLE THINGS

Things I like best
are little things,
Like baby birds
and fluffy chicks,
the puppies down the street;
A shiny rock,
My little jeep,
The buttercups we pick;
A baby calf,
Some kittens,
Our playhouse just so big.
Jesus, You were little once,
You know how it is.

GRACE BEFORE MEALS

For colours in the food we eat,
For smells that smell so good,
For things to taste and things to see,
For Mummy and Daddy
And for Thee,
Father in Heaven, we thank Thee.

Amen

THOUGHTS

I want to do
What I want,
But then I find
I don't always like
what I want.
I guess, God,
You'd better
straighten me
out.

THE BABIES WHO WOULDN'T EAT

Once a man who lived down South captured a family of five baby raccoons. He gave them plenty of food, but for days they would not eat.

To keep their pen dry, the man put their pan of water just outside the cage. The only way the little raccoons could get to the water was through a small hole in the wire. But the food on the floor of the pen lay untouched. Lumps of sugar were added to the food to tempt their appetites. Still the babies would not eat. Days passed. Their little sides were caved in with hunger.

The man was kindhearted, and he was troubled about the hungry babies. What could be wrong? Were the baby raccoons pining for their mother?

One morning he went early to the pen. As he got there, he saw one of the little raccoons pick up a lump of sugar and head for the water bowl. The raccoon pushed the sugar through the wire into the water; then he tried to put the other paw through to wash the sugar, but the hole was not large enough.

Suddenly the man knew why the babies hadn't been eating. They had simply been heeding their mother! All raccoons are taught to wash their food before eating it. The baby raccoons were ready to starve, rather than disobey.

The man rushed for a pan of water to see if he was right. This time he put it down in the middle of the pen. Right away, all five little raccoons picked up some food, headed straight for the water, washed the food thoroughly, and ate it happily.

Human children, you see, are not the only ones who have to learn to obey. Obedience is something God requires of every one of us.

THE KING
WITH WET FEET

King Canute of England lived in much splendour. Always he was surrounded by many courtiers and servants. These men thought that they could please the King by praising him.

"You are mighty and powerful," they would say.

"Nothing in all the world would dare to disobey you. Your glory will last for ever. Your kingdoms are safe from any army. You are so great that no one will take a foot of land from you."

Finally, the King grew tired of hearing all of this praise. He was a very wise King, and he knew that what his courtiers were saying just wasn't true. But he listened without saying anything.

Then one day he turned to his servants. "Bring me my great Chair of State," he ordered. When they brought the Chair of State, he said, "Now follow me, all of you, and bring the Chair of State with you."

The courtiers were greatly surprised when King Canute led them straight to the seashore.

18

The tide was out at the time. The King walked far down the beach, and ordered his chair placed at the very edge of the water, facing the sea. Then he sat down in the chair without saying another word.

Of course everyone around him wondered what he was doing, but no one dared ask the King.

After a while, the tide turned, and a little wave slipped over the sand and washed right over the Royal Feet. The courtiers' feet got wet too.

Then King Canute rose up, and stretching out his hand toward the sea, he called out in a loud and kingly voice, "This land whereon I stand is *mine.* None of the people on this land dare to resist my rule. I command thee, sea, not to mount up on my land, nor wet my feet. I command thee to retreat right away."

Just as he finished saying this, another wave — this time a big one — came hissing and foaming up the beach. This wave not only wet the Royal Feet but the Royal Ankles as well. The water poured over the

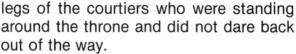

legs of the courtiers who were standing around the throne and did not dare back out of the way.

Then Canute rose again. "Let all the people on earth know," he said solemnly, "that kings have no power that God does not give them. The power of kings is vain. No one is worthy of the name of King except Him who made the land and the sea, and whose Word is the law of heaven and earth."

Then King Canute and his wet courtiers walked silently back to the town. After that no one dared to praise the King for his power and glory.

The town of Southampton, England, has been built on the very spot where this took place. There, on the wall of a little house near the docks, I have seen a small bronze plaque on which are these words:

On this spot
in 1032
King Canute rebuked
his courtiers.

GOD LOVES YOU

Said the sparrow to the robin, "I
    should really like to know
Why these anxious human beings
    rush about and worry so."
Said the robin to the sparrow, "I
    think that it must be
That they have no Heavenly Father
    such as cares for you and me."

ELIZABETH CHENEY

MANNERS

I'd be as impolite a child
As impolite could be,
To eat and quite forget to say
A thank-you, Lord, to Thee.

HAPPY EASTER!

The sun rose in a soft pink glow over the garden of Joseph of Arimathaea. Sleepy birds shook themselves awake and began to flutter and twitter. A white rabbit peered out from behind the trunk of a great tree. A dappled baby deer nuzzled her mother awake. A black sheep munched on the dew-drenched grass.

But this sunrise — so long ago — was different from any other in the world's history, for this was the dawning of the first Easter.

On Friday, Jesus had been taken down from the Cross — dead. Sorrowfully and gently, His friends had laid Him in a cave in Joseph's garden.

Now — on Easter Sunday morning — there were strange stirrings within the cave. And soon, out into the rose-tinted sunrise, walked Jesus — alive.

All the animals in the garden saw Him. Long before, at Jesus's birth, the friendly animals in the stable had been the first to welcome Him. So once again they welcomed Him, even before His human friends.

A dove settled on His shoulder and cooed her delight. The white rabbit scampered joyously around His feet. The little deer nestled close, and He smiled and stroked her dappled head. Birds circled His head, singing their happiest songs. The black sheep lay down at His feet.

Perhaps that is why the animals still help us celebrate Easter. The hen gives us her eggs to dye in rainbow colours. Fluffy yellow chickens appear in children's Easter baskets. Live bunnies with pink eyes, toy bunnies, and Easter eggs decorate the store windows.

And out on green hillsides, frisky lambs run joyously. Baby horses stand on tall, uncertain legs. Trees burst into bloom, and birds build their nests and sing happily. Each animal is saying in its own way, "We are happy because spring is here again, and love and beauty have come to earth." And because Jesus rose from the dead on that first Easter, we too are happy, for not one of us need ever be lonely or afraid again. Happy Easter!

PRAYER
FOR A SICK DOG

Dear Jesus, this is Johnny again
sending You another call for help;
I'm up in my cherry-tree house.
You seem closer up here in the sky
with green leaves and birds all around.

It's like this — my dog, Jeff, is sick.
Mummy and I have read in the Bible
about how You love little lambs,
because You're the Good Shepherd,
and about how You found the one
    lost lamb
and carried him home in Your arms
and made him well.

So we know You'll be sorry about Jeff,
    too.
Jeff doesn't want to run and play now.
His droopy ears droop more than ever.
He just looks at me with sad brown eyes
that seem to say, "Johnny, pl-ea-se
    help me."
So, dear Jesus, will You be Jeff's doctor?
And will You cure him the way
You did that baby lamb?

27

If You will, I'll nurse Jeff
and do whatever You say.
Mummy thinks the three of us
can pull him through.

He's a nice spaniel —
even if he does rumple rugs.
Anyway, I love him.
Thank You, Jesus, for listening to me.

Amen

A SMALL BOY TALKS
TO GOD

Dear God — when I was five and
    very young,
I thought all our food
came from grocery shops.
I just couldn't understand why Daddy
kept thanking You.

But now I'm six —
and much, much wiser.
Now I know that shops
would have no food, if it weren't for You,
if You didn't make things grow.

So thank You, God, for funny little seeds
that grow into pods of green peas
and red tomatoes and yellow bananas
and shiny apples.
Thank You for the rain and sunshine
to make the seeds grow.
Thank You for the farmer-men
who plant the seeds,
and for the men who drive big trucks
to take the food to market.

Thank You for shopkeepers like
    Mr. Barnes
in his big white apron,
for Daddy who buys our food,
and for Mummy, who cooks
such good things for us to eat.
Thank You, God.

Amen

SAVED BY A TAIL

Corky was a little black cocker spaniel. He was not just a make-believe dog, but a real one who lived in Winchester, Massachusetts.

One cold November day, Corky went for a walk. Soon he came to a lake named Winter Pond. The cold weather had covered Winter Pond with a thin layer of ice.

Corky walked out on the ice. But when he had reached the middle of the pond, the ice broke, and the little black dog fell into the cold water.

The little spaniel started crying and barking. Many people heard him and came running to Winter Pond. All of them wanted to rescue Corky, but they knew if they walked out on the thin ice, they, too, would fall in.

Still, Corky cried, and a big English setter heard his cries. This big dog was Corky's best friend. The big English setter raced to the edge of Winter Pond. While all the people watched, he started inching his way out on the thin ice. Very gently he put his big feet down, so the ice would not break under him.

Finally, the big dog reached Corky. He put his mouth close to Corky's ear, to tell him something important in dog-language. It must have been his plan for rescuing the little spaniel.

Then slowly, very slowly, the big dog turned around, until his long tail was right in front of the little dog's face. Corky sank his teeth in his friend's tail. When he had a firm hold, his friend began crawling towards shore. Corky hung on for dear life and was soon pulled out of the icy water. Jesus said, "Be ye kind, one to another." The big English setter knew how to be kind. He rushed to help his friend Corky when the little dog needed help. Do you watch for ways to help?

THE
BENEDICTION

And now may Almighty God
in His mercy and in His love,
Bless all those who are
near and dear to us,
In our work by day
and in our homes by night.
And keep us all in His peace
through Jesus Christ our Lord.

Amen

CUB SCOUT'S
PRAYER

Dear Father, this is Johnny talking.
Of course You know
I'm at camp.
I've tried to be good today —
and I really have had a good time.
Swimming and paddling that canoe,
and going fishing were all such fun.
I'm glad You thought
        of making cool blue water
and sunshine and silvery fish.
But, God, what about that fish
that got away?
Where did he go?
You made such pretty things, God.
I like the way the willow trees
hang over the lake.
When we paddled
        our canoe through them,
it was like being in a small green house.

I like the red of the butterfly's wings,
the funny feel
    of the dandelion flower I picked,
the big gold moon tonight,
and the feel of wiggling my toes
in the cool wet sand.
Thank You, God,
for making all these things.

Oh — and please bless Mother and Dad —
and help me to be a good scout
    tomorrow.
Good night, God.

Amen

PRAYER
FOR FORGIVENESS

Today I found my toy telephone
and I telephoned to God.
I said, "Hello, God —
are You there? How are You?
This is Johnny talking.
I want to tell You I'm sorry —
sorry about the way I acted
     this morning.
Something got into me.
It was like lions and tigers on the inside,
I'm not happy when I'm bad.

"I'm sorry for being cross to Mummy,
sorry for yelling 'no' in a scratchy voice
and banging the kitchen door.
Sorry for forgetting to feed Jeff
so that Jeff had to go away hungry.
Sorry for being mean to Betty —
She said I had a fussy forehead,
and I grabbed away my fire engine
and hurt her foot.
I *am* sorry.

39

"Daddy says the minute —
the very minute — I'm truly sorry,
and tell You what I've done wrong,
You'll forgive me.

"But I think You'd like it too,
if I tell Mummy and Betty
and Jeff that I'm sorry.
So I'll do that right now.
Then everything will be all straight again.
Good-bye — and thank You, God.

Amen."

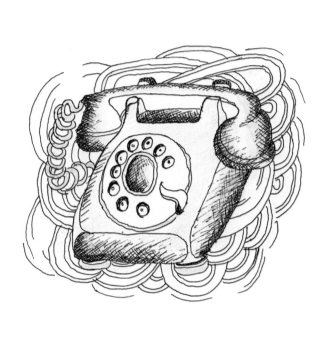

WORRY BIRDS

Lots of people pray. Then, when they have stopped praying, they keep right on worrying. But that isn't real prayer. Worry and prayer just don't mix together. Do you know why?

Suppose a boy has a broken bicycle. He takes it to a bicycle shop and asks the repairman to fix it.

The man says, "Yes, I'll fix your bike. Leave it with me. You can pick it up tomorrow afternoon."

So the boy leaves his bike and goes home. But suppose that same afternoon, the boy starts worrying. Somehow, he doesn't trust the repairman to fix his bike. What if the boy gets it into his head that the man can't do the job well? What if the boy should actually rush back to the shop and take his broken bike home, before the man has even had a chance to work on it? That would be foolish, wouldn't it? Yet, that's the way a lot of us treat God.

We ask him to fix something in our lives, or to give us something that we need very much. Then, like the little boy, we start worrying. We doubt that God can fix it. And we actually take our problem back, before He has had a chance to work on it. Worry and prayer do not go together. If you want God to fix something for you, you must trust Him. Try to trust God at least as much as you would the bicycle repairman.

THE WAY
OF A CRAB

The tide had gone out, and two crabs were strolling about on the beach.

Suddenly, one crab cried out to the other, "I don't like the way you walk. You sway from side to side. It doesn't look nice. Why don't you just walk straight forward?"

"Well," replied the other crab, "you walk straight yourself. Show me what you mean, and I'll walk just as you do."

But, as everyone knows, a crab cannot walk straight. Crabs are made so that they have to waddle from side to side.

It's a strange thing that the faults we see most clearly in other people are often the faults we have ourselves.

That's one reason why we should not find fault with other people. Don't tell anyone else to walk straight, unless you can walk straight yourself.

THEIR FACES FELL

Two workmen were fixing the roof of a house. They slipped and fell down a large chimney, landing on the floor below.
Both men scrambled to their feet, unhurt. But in the process of falling, one man had got black soot all over his face. The other man had put one arm over his face as he fell, so that his face was perfectly clean.
Now before the two men went back to work, the man with the clean face went and washed; the man with the sooty face went back to work without washing.
Can you explain why they did that?
This is a test to see how well you can think; but it is quite easy.
You see, the workmen looked at each other. The man with the clean face looked at the black face of his friend and assumed that his was sooty too.
The man with the black face saw the clean face of the other and assumed that his was clean.
Both men were wrong because they were judging themselves by each other. That is never a safe thing to do. There is only one

true standard for us to judge ourselves by. That is the perfect standard we have in Jesus.

THE GARDEN BEYOND THE GATE

Once a little boy named Andrew lived in a tiny stone cottage in the village of Dunfermline in Scotland. Andrew's father was a weaver. The family was very poor, but the tiny cottage was as clean as could be, and the bit of a garden was filled with bright flowers.

Every day on the way to school, Andrew passed some tall iron gates. He would often stop and look through the iron grillwork. Beyond, there was a great house surrounded by rolling green lawns and beautiful gardens. And out beyond the house there was a little valley, called Pittencrieff Glen, through which a singing stream wound its way.

But the gates were always closed, and the little boy could never go in.

"When I grow up, if I make a lot of money," Andrew often said to himself, "I'll buy that beautiful park. Then I'll open the gates wide and invite all the children in the town to play inside. When I own it, the gates will never be locked again."

48

When he was thirteen, Andrew's family sold everything they owned in Scotland and moved to America. They went to Pittsburgh. There young Andrew started to work as a bobbin boy in a cotton factory. He didn't earn much, but it was not long before he was earning more.

Indeed, Andrew seemed to have been given the gift of knowing how to make money. As the years went by he became very rich.

When some people get a great deal of money, they want to keep all of it for themselves. But Andrew found that it was fun to share.

So he built libraries and concert halls; he gave parks and organs; he gave money to colleges and universities. He gave away money to work towards peace and to reward men for acts of courage and bravery.

In the year 1868, Andrew and his mother went back to Scotland on a visit. Andrew had not forgotten about that little boy peering through the tall iron gates, nor had he forgotten the promises he had made to himself. He had seen many beautiful places in the world, but the park behind the iron gates in his own town in Scotland still seemed the most beautiful of all.

So he bought it, and right away he opened the gates and gave the park to the people of Dunfermline. Ever after the children have run and laughed and played in Andrew Carnegie's beautiful park. And each year — in August — when flowers are at their loveliest, all the school children have a picnic there. Not a single one is left out.

THE COMING OF THE KING

One day a long time ago, some children were playing in their playground, when a herald rode through the town, blowing a trumpet and shouting, "The King! The King will pass along this road today. Make ready for the King!"

The children stopped playing and looked at one another. "Did you hear that?" one asked.

"The King is coming," said another. "He might look over the wall and see our playground. It's messy. We must make it all nice and neat for him."

The playground was indeed messy. Broken toys lay all around. There were scraps of paper on the ground. The children had a lot of work to do before it was tidied and looked really neat again.

"Now it looks better," one child said. "But kings are used to such fine things. Let's make it pretty."

So the children gathered green, sweet-smelling branches and scattered them on the ground. They brought leaves and fresh ferns and hung them on the wall. One little boy picked marigolds and threw them on the ground. "To make it look like gold," he said.

When they had finished, the playground looked so beautiful that the children just stood and looked at it.

"Let's keep it like this always," one said, clapping her hands with delight.

"Yes, that's just what we'll do," everyone shouted.

The children waited all day for the coming of the King, but he didn't come. Towards evening, though, just as the sun was setting, an old man with travel-worn clothes and a kind, tired face passed along the road and stopped to look over the wall.

"What a pretty place," the old man said.

"May I come in and rest?"

"Oh, yes," the children said. So they brought him in and helped him to a seat they had made of an old barrel. They had covered the barrel with a red cloak to make it look like a throne. It made a fine throne.

"This is our playground," one little boy said. "We made it all pretty for the King, but he never came. But we are going to keep it pretty always in case he does come."

The gentle old man sat and rested. He smiled at the children with such kind eyes that they gathered around him and told him their best secrets — about the five puppies in the barn, about the tree where the robin's nest with the blue eggs was, and about the seashore where the golden shells grew. And the man nodded and understood it all.

After a while, the man asked for a cup of cool water, so the children brought it to him in their best, clean tin cup. They were very kind to the stranger.

Then the old man thanked the children and rose to go. But before he left, he laid his hands on their heads, and each child felt a warm thrill as he did so.

The children stood by the wall and waved to him as he went slowly down the road.

The sun was setting, and the golden light fell in long slanting rays across the road. "He looked so tired," said one of them.

"But he was so nice," said another.

"See," said the smallest child, "see how the sun shines on his hair! It looks like a golden crown."

Maybe — maybe the man was the King after all.

Now King Jesus has come to earth. And He has promised us, "Lo, I am with you always. ..."

We can't see Him with our eyes, but we can feel His presence in our hearts. Do you try to make your work and play fine enough to please the King?

CHRISTMAS LIGHTS

O starlight from the singing sky,
Starlight, come to earth!
Blazon every fragrant tree,
Shine in children's eyes, that we
May kneel to love the Baby King.

O starlight from the singing sky,
Come swiftly now to earth!
Shine in every darkened place,
Capture every land and race,
Till children everywhere can bring
Happy gifts to praise the King.

MORNING

The stars are gone,
The silver moon is hiding
from the sun.
A merry bird
just called to me,
"Wake up, the day's begun."
Good morning, World!
Good morning, God!

NIGHT

Tonight the earth
is crowned with stars,
a soft wind hums a tune,
And for a hat
the pine tree wears
a slice of saucy moon.
Good night, World!
Good night, God!